Sweetwater, Saltwater

*For Tony & Gundi
with warm regards
Rosalie*

Sweetwater, Saltwater

poems by
Rosie King

Hummingbird Press
Santa Cruz, California

Copyright c 2007 by Rosie King

All rights reserved. No part of this book may be reproduced in any manner without permission in writing, except for brief quotations in reviews or articles.

Library of Congress Control Number: 2007920368
ISBN #13: 978-0-9792567-0-7 ISBN #10: 0-9792567-0-4

Acknowledgement is made to the following publications for poems originally appearing in them, usually in an earlier version:

California Quarterly, "After Breaking the Butter Dish," "The Young Bougainvillea"; *In Celebration of the Muse*, "The Child Coming Toward Her"; *Lighthouse Point*, "Summer Nights on the River Island"; *Northwest Poets and Artists Calendar*, "And the Spirits of the Earth Said"; *Quarry West*, "Midsummer Homecoming."

The author also thanks warmly for their friendship and encouragement: Tom and Carol King, C.G. and Pam King, Rosalie Riegle, Ginny Anderson Nash, Nan Spence, Judith Jordan, Patricia Hannum, Jim and Sharon Murfin, Christine Nagel, Molly Jones, Kitty Washburn, Jo Muilenberg, Jan and Mesa Broek, Joel Dorius, Robin and Linda Gajdusek, John Weir Perry, Paula Kimbro, Sara Webb, Bill Samsel, Marion Rosen and the Rosen community; Toni Packer and friends from Santa Sabina; Lew Fein, Dale Strawhacker, Ed Smyth, Tilly Shaw, Barbara Hull, Naomi Clark, Sharman Murphy, Roz Spafford, Charles Atkinson, Ken Weisner, David Sullivan, Debra Spencer, Anita Wilkins, Mary Lonnberg Smith, Barbara Bloom, Paula Jones, Joseph Stroud and poets in the ongoing group; Joan Zimmerman, Joan Safajek, John and Wilma Chandler, Gary Upham, Robert Sward and Gloria Alford, Lynn Luria-Sukenick, Carolyn Burke, Gaza Bowen, Ann Barros, Kathleen Roberts, Kofi Busia, Maya Lev and yoga friends; Carolyn Atkinson, Katherine Thanas, Edward Brown, Michael Sawyer, Gaelyn Godwin, Reb Anderson and friends from Green Gulch/Tassajara/San Francisco Zen Center; Len Anderson, and all the *Hummingbird* poets, founding and new.
In memory of Carl Gray King and Violet Nagel King.

Cover, frontispiece, and author photos by Paula Kimbro
Graphic design by Kathleen Roberts
InDesign by Ken Weisner and David Sullivan

HUMMINGBIRD PRESS
2299 Mattison Lane
Santa Cruz, CA
95062-1821

Printed by Bookmobile

for all my loved ones

CONTENTS

And the Spirits of the Earth Said   9

I. The Arrow, Bright Green
Midsummer Homecoming   13
Summer Nights on the River Island   14
Rain Song   15
The Young Bougainvillea   17
When It Would Not End   18
All the Years Since Our Parting, All the Bright Colors   20
Persimmons   22
The Leopard   23
When Everything Seemed Possible   24
Sculpting the Angel   25
Imagine Being Voiceless Forever   26
Light and Dark, Front and Back Foot Walking   27

II. My Bones
After I Bring My Wedding Dress Home   31
Dark Horse   34
Calling Out to You   36
Night Vision   37
Blue Giraffe   38
After Breaking the Butter Dish   40
The Child Coming Toward Her   41
Sweetwater, Saltwater   43
Child Slipping Away   45
End of a Moon   46
Mother's Day
   48
Visitation   50
Mid-November Snow   51
Midwinter   53

III. After a Long Time in the Mountains

Dodonaea	57
After a Long Time in the Mountains	58
This Bright Cold, Your Birthday	59
"As a blue channel of sky opens"	60
Santa Sabina, Six Days of Rain	61
In the Night	62
Before We Knew of Parting	63
Six a.m.	64
In the Raspberry Patch	65
The Blue Sky at Pinnacles Again	66
After Three Thousand Saturdays	67
Finishing	68
After Turning off the News of War	69
Night Heron	70
Rest in This	72
In the Blink of an Eye	73
Saturdays	74
After Miss Shelley, Miss Hattersley, Miss Guilford	75
Old South School	76
Killarney Beach	77

IV. The Root Tree Dreams

Night After Night	81
The Root Tree Dreams	82
Rowboat	93
The Deer at Santa Sabina	94

And the Spirits of the Earth Said

*We come up out of the dark full of bees
we call your name slowly
with fires
with a white feather
we wipe you clean as glass
we give you the smallest bird
a seed open and closing
a pulse in your hand*

I.

The Arrow, Bright Green

Midsummer Homecoming
for my mother

It was the summer of the landing on the moon.
I remember my weariness arriving after dark,
the balmy air blowing over the bay,
the cottage with the sloping roof
and how we climbed the stairs.
You had prepared my room—
fresh sheets, the windows open wide—
where all night long the lapping of the waves
cradled my sleep, and the wind billowed the curtains,
pink gauze in the moonlight,
promising, promising.
                                       Melons at breakfast,
honeyrock and honeydew, and then the gathering
of shells, the long sun-baths.
                                Time is going fast,
you told me (you who'd picked the rose
for the bud-vase), was it late afternoon?
One boy playing tennis
had black curly hair and I
still so hungry
for the boy running up from the field saying *Rosie, Rosie,*
summers before,
and no words could tell you
all that drew me home,
or how I wanted time to be
turned back, so I could still be floating,
the way the moon once was,
waiting to be touched.

Summer Nights on the River Island

At bedtime I asked them,
the cousins younger than I.
We were up in the cubbyholes
under the eaves, with the old bear-rug smell
and the sound of pigeons cooing.
I carried them,
their smooth young bodies hugging mine,
fresh after baths, or warm from hide-and-seek,
tucked them in still nuzzling,
and as they fell asleep
urged them
Can you remember
what it was like
before you were born?
as if their newer flesh must hold the secret
mine had lost.
Though their bodies pulsed with it,
I needed them to speak.
I was listening from a far edge of childhood
where the moon-shadows lengthened,
and the night grew huge
with every rustle of leaf
and even the island was held
deep in the river-bed.

Rain Song
for a child longed for

On a wet day
you want me to speak of earlier rains.
So I take you back
to the break in the hedge under the rose arbor,
white trellis arching up over the path,
old stone pieces, dark green leaves,
and the small roses climbing.

I take you back
under the rose arbor, the way through
to the backyard with the cherry tree—
up a ladder, in the branches,
mouths and buckets full of sweet bright fruit.

I show you the house we lived in,
high and white like a castle on the corner,
the stone lions guarding their urns of geraniums,
my mother in her garden,
violets and lilies, spring
mornings after rain. Summer
and the mourning dove's early
song in the deep shade of the willow,
the peonies by the driveway
blooming always on my brother's birthday.

You want to know how I could ever leave.
I tell you how the clouds moved
more and more slowly, how I knew
the willow's every branching,
how the hiding places in the berry bushes
vanished, and—like a bird

whose song, *Who am I? Who
am I?*, pressed up in her throat—
I knew I had to fly.

The Young Bougainvillea

Laughter and honey keep us in bed all morning.
At noon the spider comes dangling
down a long thread,
finds us weeping in our bare bodies,
the whole day caved in between us,
and nothing to do beyond rising.

Lemons and plums by the window,
a long look out to the crow,
somebody singing in the shower next door—
could we be making it all up?
The arrow you drew on your arm, bright green,
points to the young bougainvillea.
I say nobody will ever find us here.
You will still have to leave.
Just look how the table is round,
smooth bare pine, how the grain swirls.

Night comes out of the sky in a rush of black wings—
time is slipping away, I know
I will never live here again
and one day barely remember.

When It Would Not End

        I.
You took me to the hillside.
It was no longer green.
Blood-red, the maple leaves
low in the thickets.
And in the throat
still the love-words
hooked.
        Your shadow fell
over me, the blue sky
hid, and I heard only
the leaves of a storm
I wanted to tie to your shoulder,
give them up to you
wild-tossing,
give my face
up to you
under brush
where I could not speak
and the leaves
spread like hands.

It happened
so quickly,
the tongues licking
the thighs on fire.
O be sweet,
be slow,
make us new.

Find me, find me,
cried an old fear
of being left, of being lost.

II.
Then one we knew
troubled and bright
put a shotgun
to his heart.

That longest night
I kept waking.
Cold in your house.
I was sleeping in the sewing room
on the high, hard bed,
your wife, my good friend,
gone up to bed early.
*So much perfection,
and so much waste,* you said.

Who could have known
we'd need more
than comfort?

And be found,
deep in the night
where no word could save us, aching.

All the Years Since Our Parting, All the Bright Colors

     I.
I'm alone in your house on a hill, all white
inside, waiting for you. I don't want to be there,
my whole body slanting down the long steps.
I see you in the distance,
at the end of the circular driveway.
It's almost Christmas, your arms are full of packages,
your wife is still my friend, dear to me,
coming home with you across the lawn.
I'm holding the door open.

     II.
Your son will soon be twelve;
he turns his face,
slips by me in the hall.
He's not the child I knew.
I want to call out to him,
"Remember when you were five
and showed me the red eggs at Easter?
We have to say dyeing THEM, you said,
or else it means
when we stop breathing."

     III.
You take me to the museum,
and there, in the sunny courtyard,
near the chamber of the sculptures of lovers,
you kiss me over and over.
Your face is radiant; how lightly
the air moves! Your wife
comes to sit in my lap,
her belly is round where I hold her,
and the pale woman in gray
who slips in by the side door
saying *no, no,* cannot part us.

IV.

On the shortest day of the year, you call. I am
wearing bright red and blue. This is
not a dream. Your voice
buries everything I want to say.
I completely forget
to tell you—in my last dream
we were climbing, somewhere in rock
or snow, a zig-zag trail, you behind me,
breathing hard. *Slow down*,
you called. I saw you wince, and then
slump to the ground—
I cried in the night at that sudden waking,
my heart racing,
as if it beats with yours.

Persimmons
for Rosie Sieracki Hull (1952-1989)

We ran in a field of black ponies.
And now I feel loved again. You would understand this,
you who once could feel the joy of your breathing.
As I lie here this morning, each breath
is new and delights me,
the air is cool from the open window
and the sun, just rising,
shines across the bay in a light rain.
All the green leaves glisten,
and as I rise, the cool air follows me.

When I stand in the kitchen, I can see the persimmons,
deep orange and ripening in their row on the sill,
each shining with its one intense spot of sunlight,
clear as in a child's painting,
each with its shadow side
and with its shadow under it.

The sun also shines
deep in the red bowl you gave me.
A few days ago, as I rinsed it clean,
I saw your face, the sun still catching your blond hair.
It was that very hour you were parting
from your sisters, your young sons, your husband—
gone beyond the field of black ponies
as I filled the red bowl with autumn fruit,
not yet knowing.

The Leopard
for Grace Dooseman (1959-1984)

In that first class I taught, where all
the girls had beautiful names,
across the round table you were Grace,
your poems filled with spices and roses.
These are your legs, your leaps, you wrote,
light comes through the windows
. . . you have a body and are glad for it.
And yet, that week before my wedding,
you took your life.

Now these first spring rains,
I go looking in a box, in a basket,
gathering up the notes and cards from you,
open one to find you rejoicing in New York—
To be young and supple, up late at night.
And yet, from a page in your journal,
a baboon being chased by a leopard—*no trees,*
no trees to climb into . . .
                    no medicine
for the wrinkled baby, my lost brother,
my still young parents in hiding from the Nazis . . .
on V-Day, walking out slowly to sit by the roadside
where my mother gathers flowers.

On May Day, other students led
as we climbed the ladder into the redwood—
you sat below, a hundred branches down
where light filtered softly.
We left you with strawberries.
You opened a book.
Your voice drifted up to us.

When Everything Seemed Possible
for Lynn

I was looking for a dime
in the ladies' room at the airport
when you walked in glowing
your I-know-a-secret smile.
You asked for a lemon life-saver.
From my mouthful of silver
I lent you a quarter. Then you told me:
The man who waits for me
wears a golden skull-cap. He's
a prince from Africa who hums in my ear.

High up in the hotel suite we unfurled his gift,
a quilt of many textures,
filling the room with embroidered colors
and, branching from its sky-blue edges,
unfinished pieces, the pattern still growing—
trees with apples, pears,
pomegranates bearing their honeycombs
of crimson seeds.   I wanted us to eat them
with the whole globe split open in the light
and shared, as we did in those dazzling conversations
when everything seemed possible—
before the blight of anger
that came flashing out of your dying.

Sculpting the Angel
for Robert Duncan

Angels we talked about, climbing the coast,
the curve up Skyline, brightest blue.
Gabriel, Raphael, the Elohim!

We said guardian angels are intimate—
presences we called them, intensities . . .
as at Luxor by the Nile
where H.D. first saw
those giant carvings of the bee.

At the door of your house,
steep steps and the stained glass windows,
we laughed when we shook hands twice.

I returned across the bridge . . .
when in the company of the gods
I loved and was loved . . .

O clouds, I say this darker day-after,
filter the light back softly.
Let me see this thing I am shaping,
sinew and bone—
eye-socket shining!

Imagine Being Voiceless Forever

A way to speak may surprise you
like the web in the night
when you rise for a glass of water—
skin tingles all through the house.

Where have you been? Flying,
the book of the muse in your arms?
Can you find your way back in the dark?
This is the candle, here by the bed.

And the thirst that woke you?
Just listen.
These are the deep night sounds:
waves' roar
and your love's soft breathing.

Light and Dark, Front and Back Foot Walking

A blaze of sun—
we stretch out naked,
skin to granite, soaking up the heat.
This is the creek I imagined.

Pine shadows lengthen in the pool,
skater-bugs on the water.
We slip in, the shadows
flicker on our bodies.

And then comes a wind,
shivering leaves,
darkening water.
A hawk flies, wings beating fast.

Inside our tent
we touch, our bodies limber,
fire kindles,
and we love that heat.

When a low gruffle wakes us,
we leap out, banging our cook-pans
into the dark and under the spinning
billions of stars

to meet the black glow
and glitter of eyes—
the slow-swaying
head of bear.

II.

My Bones

After I Bring My Wedding Dress Home

I.
My grandmother rises up out of her rocker,
opens a cupboard, pushes aside her butter churn and biscuit cutter,
quilting scissors, thimble and thread,
gives me the blue glass jar we took firefly catching
summers on the Culleoka farm.
Culleoka, she whispers in the dream,
clear water.

II.
At sixty, in a heat wave after canning season,
my grandmother came in and put a match to the drapes,
white lace billowing up, my grandfather running hard
up the hill from his mules.

He took her himself. Oatfield, wheatfield,
alfalfa, corn. Fifty-five miles
to the hospital in Nashville.
1947. Shock

treatments, hot baths,
her gold wedding ring
stolen, never found.
The weather

cooled, a remarkable
change—
more like herself.
And then the move to town.

III.
That house, the hard-water smell
of the upstairs bathroom, yellow linoleum,
curled-under feet on the tub.

My stubborn handsome grandfather,
bellowing from the bottom of the stairs
Alllll right! to wake us.
Be sweet, my grandmother'd tell us at breakfast.

    IV.
Depression: sunk
below its surroundings,
a hollow. What she'd
fallen into.

What he'd lost his shirt in.
What happened
when you got married
down South,

had babies,
moved from farm to farm—
hay to haul,
hogs to slaughter,

canning, pickling, pressure-
cooking, daughters vowing
never marry a farmer,
sons, *never be one.*

    V.
What happened came
filtered, through others,
in whispers
over the years:
drop of fear,
drop of fear.

Once she was a girl, like me—
what happened to her?

Nobody wants to ask,
nobody wants to say.
Wisp of a smile,
cat got her tongue,
she looks all thrown away.

The grandmother I last knew
just sitting there at eighty, shapeless
in her housedress,
clammed up.

    VI.
I dream a doctor slaps her dead cheeks, opens her jaws,
begins to pump her stomach
for the embalming—
                        she comes back to life a young woman,
dark brown hair piled high
as in her bridal picture,
while underneath the lace of her wedding dress
she wears the plain white shift
of the hospital room.

Still she holds the firefly jar
and in my ear she whispers
Culleoka, clear water.

Dark Horse
for my father at 78

October night, leaving you there, high up in the hospital,
we saw the geese flying south in the moonlight.
Tomorrow your heart would lie open.

I dreamed the tree-men came in the night.
I saw their lanterns flicker,
the shadows of their long axes
battle the branches we'd climbed, that canopy
with its many slim leaves that once
fluttered over our birthdays—they cut
our old willow down to the ground.

When I turned to look again
it was alive in the dawn-wind, spreading wide
its green-gold streamers, sheltering the yard.

In your dream, the summer before,
you were cleaning out your desk at the office,
the way you'd been meaning to for weeks,
just getting started with the paper clips and pennies.
Suddenly the desk was in the tack-room at our old farm.
You heard a little nicker and then who

came ambling by the window
but Shad, old horse-trainer you'd loved,
so you called out, *Hey, Shad, who's that nicker from?*

And Shad, in that voice
slow like yours, chuckled, *Mister King,
we done sold all but one. This one's
something special. I been saving him.
Onliest one who'll see him is the one who gets around me
and sneaks a look.*

So that was the risk you took
that long quarter hour your heart
stopped beating—and the surgeons, the stooped one,
the young one from horse country, marveled
how you came back, a dark horse,
the surprise of your life.

Calling Out To You
in your eightieth year

Here at the edge of the meadow
I watch you swim across the clear lake.
You're my young mother,
                             your face
a bloom among the lilies
and the lily-pads.
                 You lift your arms;
your body ripples through the water.

On the far side, where the woods begin,
you look so much smaller. You try
to pull yourself up; the steep bank
crumbles in your hands.
                     I think of
diving in—your arms would flail,
pull me under.
               I call out—
can you hear me
running with my brothers,
our feet thudding
bare on the path?
                How can it be
that the rim of the earth will not hold you?

Night Vision

It happens in an ancient country:
someone has taken our picture—
two old people and a daughter
climbing the monument, stone steps
that fade into the distance.

I stand in the bottom left corner
holding you, my mother, where you've fallen
down into my arms. You are so small,
like the mummy of a child,
your arms wrapped closely
around your breasts, your heart.
My open mouth cries—

while you, my father,
still climb slowly, far up.
Be careful, I call out.
I can barely see your shoulders curve,
your head just nodding.
I know you hear me
as step by step
you near the edge of the picture.

Blue Giraffe
for my father

In the shadow of the bank building
where the wind flapped your hat
you'd take me up and up
and I'd ride your shoulder past the green light
to eat mashed potatoes in the Bancroft Hotel.
If my head bumped a corner, you'd kiss it;
when I lost my blue giraffe,
you found it.

Now, in your winter dream,
hoodlums take you underground,
your old heart pounding,
just tunnels of ice, jagged chunks that shift and crash
as if the whole conglomerate of cold
were caving in on top of you.
It seems to go on all night,
not knowing where they're going to dump you.
You shiver a little as you tell me,
while I, at your bedside,
pull the quilt closer.

I want to say, remember
when you were a farm-boy
chopping firewood with your grand-dad,
that hill where the spring came out of a cave,

your mouth watering for the musk-melons he'd stashed there.
You grew up, left that woodlot and your ax,
made your passage beyond those woods,
went far north—and then, remember,
you took us back to that Culleoka farm,
summer evening coming on,
Nanny in her white chair, all of us

out in the yard eating melons,
and up in the tree-shadows,
fireflies . . .

Silently, to the night-light,
to the wind blowing snow past the window,
I say all this, and more,
as you go down into sleep, your face
changing back into a boy's.

After Breaking the Butter Dish

Now I can never give it to a daughter.
I sit down in the middle of the living room floor
and remember my grandmother, and her mother,
homemade bread and rolls and butter
and how many tables with that dish on it,
and imagine saying *handed down from your great-great-grandmother.*

How early it was, Valentine's Day, and raining.
It felt like a morning for soaking some beans,
pouring them into the strainer,
no place to put the empty jar
and then my arm just barely brushing.
O crystal dome with the bird on top—smashed.

I know what you want to tell me. Are you
the smallest bird in the poem I was writing
Valentine's Day three years ago coming home?
Are you the egg-bird on the postcard?
Are you the robin
the girl is looking up to
in the old picture?

Well, now nobody else can break you;
my cousin won't be nervous around you.
I get my glasses, go back to the kitchen,
sweep it all up. I save the bird,
and smash a little of the glass around the bottom
so it can sit without falling over.
I am almost too old to have a daughter.

The Child Coming Toward Her
*I go where I love and am loved
into the snow* —H.D.

December, years later,
an emptiness, an oldness.
I don't know where to look.
You'd think there'd be a landmark,
some rock or tree, something
to stroke the fingers over.
So easily we lose the way.

I want to go back there
into that dark time
of cold winter waking
when the day broke in pieces,
dry cold, late November, walking
block after block of dry leaves.
The men at the half-way house
sat in rockers reading papers.
It seemed important to keep moving.

When the snow came,
all the colors were gone
except blue sky and evergreen.
Too far north to open windows.
Still I kept wanting to.

Then you who'd lived there longest,
ranch girl, my brother's love,
brought home the bird book
and we made our own oriole,
robin, hummingbird, jay—
painted beaks and feathers and eyes
on all their baked-dough shapes.
They hung on the tree—it was almost Christmas—
that night we heard of the young woman dying.

You my brother, her pastor, came home to tell us
how, in her vision
the child she had been was the child coming toward her,
the same dark curls, in a halo of light—
and I, too, became a child again.

I remembered the nights
before Christmas, before our birthdays,
when looking up at the star-field
we could ride far out into time
and never be lost . . .
and I saw in the window
our candlelit birds flashing—
blue spruce,
dark bloom of new light.

for Tom and Carol

Sweetwater, Saltwater

I.
1901. Hot summer when my grandparents met, a Great Lakes
Fourth of July—families and picnics off to the bay, the train
stalled on the track, young Bill running through the coach
where Clara sat, sixteen in her ruffled shirtwaist,
the prettiest one, laughing with her sisters
when from under that tall straw hat
his glasses fell in her lap.

All those summers the children grew.
They'd take the train to Bayport, open the cottage,
let it fill with the breeze off that sweetwater bay
and ease into the long days— tracking sand in, napping,
waking to a rowboat knocking.

Clara took the pictures: her Bill in the reeds, pulling the boat in;
Harold on horseback out in the waves;
Violet, my mother, laughing from her sandbar;
Billy, still a towhead, fishing off the dock—
If wishes were fishes she wrote on that one.

The lavender scent of her
bending over me when I was the child
she lulled to sleep, the waves lapping.
Her cottage at Linwood, wide-porched and wickered,
its dock with a ladder, its dapple of leaves and birdbath
in clover. I banged a pail and learned to walk,
and Hans the boxer, patient prince,
let me put my hand in his slobbery mouth.

My grandmother sold the cottage at Linwood
to Frank Starkweather's grandmother over the bridge table.
That was after she'd almost died at forty-eight
of a burst appendix in the days before penicillin.

Only sips of the finest champagne, said the doctor.
She kept the Tiffany lamp and her favorite wicker,
left behind the white baby grand.

Summers later, she taught me to knit and embroider
on the screened porch of her house on Wheeler.
Hands that had once played Chopin
knew patience with knots, slipped stitches.
I'd ride my bike the two blocks around the corner,
past the stone deer and the grape arbor. Cool
on the screened porch, iced tea with fresh mint.

    II.
I sit on a stump, cracking sticks—
eucalyptus and Monterey pine for kindling.
Hot, even in the shade.
No breeze off this bay.
Saltwater I'm still not used to:
the thrill of being buoyed up,
the sting if there's a wound.

Along this saltwater beach
I walked a month,
a sea-change inside,
murmuring *Clara, Will,*
wishing *girl, boy*—a last chance,
so close, the sweet surge of my body
already rounding.

Child Slipping Away
for Judith

You've sent me a card of Gauguin's
Tahitian Women Bathing, the same
oranges as the fishes
rising from our pond
to mouth their food.
In the ripples
fins flash,
reddest tangerine.

You give me back
that summer of our long visit—
my *calm beauty and warm radiance*
inspired you in your mothering.

In the pool
around our hips, by turns,
your slippery youngest,
frog-legs squirming,
first thrill of going under
and coming up again
to breathe.

I dip my fingers
for the carp to suckle.

Back then
we held the world afloat,
all that mother-juice, flowing in you,
ripening in me
as in a late orange on the tree—
sun-drenched,
getting sweeter.

End of a Moon
for my mother, turning eighty

      I.
When you come to visit, I tie the silk scarf
under your chin and we go out,
walking the neighborhood slowly,
noticing the flowers, the cats
and the birds. Of course you are talking.
Mostly you can't get over
the way cats keep following you.
They seem to know they spook me, you say.

I want to tell you how we took turns
in anatomy class, tenderly cutting
a cat, the intricate patterns of vein, membrane and muscle.
Inside: the heart, lungs, intestines curling,
and the womb with its tendrils of ovaries.
Are you with me?
We're on our way home now.

      II.
One night, bright fur in the headlights' glare
squiggled back into their nest in our garage.
Who knows why the cat came to us with kittens?
We'd just given away all the books on childbirth.
Skinny dark calico.   I feel her bones.
We add butter to the milk; she drinks it all.

      III.
I fly to be with you.
Walk, says the doctor.
They've taken your womb
and used it to patch your bladder.

You're sleeping when Ed calls—
the wild mother cat
run over in the night.
Let it be, you say.

How many times I've wept, knowing
no child will come from my womb.

I walk out into the dark,
the end of a moon—
air fresh, rain in the grass.
The kittens will find a home, you'd say.

Mother's Day

Three shades of pink cut-out hearts
and a butterfly:

*For a Very
Special Daughter
on Mother's Day.*

My name on the envelope
in my father's now spidery hand.
Inside, under the verse,
her handwriting, quavery as his:

*I am just happy I am
a mother and have a
daughter like you.*

How many springs ago now,
that rush of new life
slipping away?
I know I must be over it
because I'm not crying.

I just ran across it, his note explains.
*She must have picked it out last spring,
wrote in it, then forgot to send it.*

My mother who can't remember
what year or month or day it is,
standing in front of the greeting cards.

Why not? I can hear her saying,
reaching out for the card, her most
daring love note, before she forgets—

as if she'd planned it to arrive
when the worst of the ache is over.

So what if there's been no baby?
Who else would think of it?
A Mother's Day card—
my first. From anybody.

Visitation

We dress you in purple silk,
pearls in gold shells at your ears.

We sing to you, pray
to be led *beside the still waters.*

At nightfall, as we leave you,
rain pours over black umbrellas.

One grandchild, tall as her mother,
stands on the steps holding lilies,

her own face
wet with rain,

her own way of looking
into the night: *free . . .*

you're free now,
she murmurs;

lightly, in the marrow,
she carries you.

Mid-November Snow
for my father (1907-1997)

In the Oscoda woods, sun sparking
off new-fallen snow, the hush
of the wild held my brother Carl,
hunkered down behind brush
with his gun, waiting
for the buck's antlers
to pierce the blue.

In the hunting cabin, the phone was ringing.

> *You'd hugged your son, told him to go,*
> *not to miss the hunt.*

In Missoula, ice on the Clark Fork,
my brother Tom walked his dogs
past the park and the tiny burr oak
with its plaque for our mother.

> *Frail, past ninety,*
> *in a house near the old farm you loved.*

In the Santa Lucias, I hiked up the creek-canyon,
and near the summit, storm clouds clearing,
an enormous live-oak,
maybe the oldest anywhere.

> *Snow drifting to the doorstep,*
> *a caregiver held you.*

My flight carries the shadow of the plane
over cloudfields, snowfields,
slow descent, through spiral
after spiral of rainbows.

At the landing, both my brothers waiting.
Snowflakes melt on their overcoats.

*The first long moments by your casket,
a sense of you so keen it looks like breathing.*

*Then only my own breath
and the piercing snow.*

Midwinter

I pause in the dark
on the stairs to my house.
Above me, shadowy on the railing,
three owls—all heartbeat and breathing.
They've come in winter,
in drought.

There will be no child.

I stretch out my hand
in the way of the falconer,
my left hand and wrist,
arm from the heart.
Their quick claws.
Their beaks click.
I hear in their ruffle of feathers,

Let your arm lift
like a wing.

III.

After a Long Time in the Mountains

Dodonaea

The winter storms shook you,
purple-leafed tree, bent you even more,
all these years leaning east—
now your trunk crushes the ivy hedge,
the weight of your crown
against a neighbor's peaked roof.
We could put in a big stake by the hedge,
says the arborist, *tether it back.*
But how undignified.

Mere shrub when I moved here.
Hopseed, supposed to be a bush.
We marvel—your many-branched crown high as my roof.
I've loved your royal flirting at my bedroom window—
flashes of purple rustles in the night.
Your kind flourishes here,
full sun by the ocean.
Maybe one day
I'll have another—who knows?
You're felled. Days go by.
There's a hole in space.

Then spring above the rooftops—
scarlet swoop of a kite,
fast-flying line of the first brown pelicans—
not ready, yet here I am,
flinging open the window,
glad for more sky.

After a Long Time in the Mountains

I'm swimming my own stretch of beach again
as the tidal wave grows
over my shoulder, then I'm diving

deep under, shoreward,
making great swoops of breaststroke and frog-kick,
skimming along the rippled sandy bottom.

Here sea-light billows, pearly
and golden, and I'm breathing easily underwater
all the way to shore

to land dripping with sea-foam, to your doorstep—
and you open the door, poet of my youth, still so fresh-eyed.
I could stay—

yet the dream has its own way,
lifts us
floating down among the sycamores, umbrellas,

to stroll awhile.
I hear a stumble beside us, reach
for that curly-haired mystic, balding and stooped,

beloved irrepressible,
our hands warming his breast-bone and back
until he breathes easily.

I know,
after such a long time away,
having plunged so deep—

whether our hands
will ever meet as lovers,
whether yearning could ever be over—

this touching keeps us close to the mountains.

This Bright Cold, Your Birthday
for Ed

I seem to be rolling out pie dough,
opening cans of cherries, mostly tart
the way you liked them, mixed with sweet dark Bings
and golden Queen Annes.
We must be back in our old house.

Out beyond the cypress, the waves are scalloped—
the hems of wedding dresses—
tossing their white ruffles.
The pie's in the oven,
plumped in its deep dish,
foil around the crust.

You show me page after page
in a notebook, long passages, all dated.
Before I can speak, you're down the steps,
walking away, backwards at first, your right hand
holding up a set of keys, your left a small
jug of maple syrup, the shape somehow familiar—

and then I'm waking to the bitter-sweetness
of your leaving,
to these wild peaks of the Santa Lucia,
to sun that glints off white creek-water,
to cold so bright the mind clears.

Tassajara, February 1998

"As a blue channel of sky opens..."
Mary Lonnberg Smith (1939—1983)

A hummingbird, ruby-throated,
whirs among the roses— I hear your voice

as if you were still arriving,
striding through Tilly's gate

in gleeful mid-sentence... *God!*
... *hid-eous!*—

nothing held back.
Then the house grew quiet,

the books flared open
to the wild geese of Hiroshige.

The calendar tells me.
This day in August.

You were traveling east toward mountains you loved
when a truck...

That sudden.
But did you glimpse

past it?   Did you know more
in the rush of that moment

than your poems
had already told us

of the climb over high passes,
the pure air,

the longing ... the updraft
and downsweep of wings?

Santa Sabina, Six Days of Rain

Mud underfoot and the slippery leaves,
torn streamers of bark—eucalyptus.
I long to touch each naked trunk,
uplifting, shedding its skin.

Keep climbing, to the crest of open sky,
the live-oak, its wild limbs.
I want to stay forever, arms around a low branch.
From above a drop falls—
catch it on my tongue,
all I'll ever need.

Still, the manzanita
stops me—its trunk's
whole length ripped open,
a writhing core—
at the top, new shoots,
green leaves burst out,
alive, alive!
and I stand here
in my body
growing old.

In the Night

At a bookshop,
the high-boned face I knew,

the hand reaching out, warm and full
clasping mine. Twice

he gave it,
in greeting and in parting,

so the warmth
came home with me,

and still in the care of it,
I went

to bed,
at first not knowing why

I lay there weeping.

Before We Knew of Parting

We woke up running for the open window
where blowing rain flung
loose strands of curtain, and the cobalt bowl
rang like a gong—all our art books,
edges dripping. A sponge,
a dry cloth, each one opened,
until they all stood on edge,
pages fanned out.

In those light spring days
before we knew of parting,
we kept them spread out by the sunny window.
Timeless together—
Rodin lovers, Degas dancers,
the Unicorn and his Lady.
Their vivid colors held us.
Hatshepsut on her Throne,
The Noble Scholar under a Willow.

Six a.m.

Whoo-whoo of mourning doves,
rumble of waves, this early sweet patter—and I'm up
plunging night clothes still warm into rain pants
and slicker, boots by the door, out
to pull a tarp over the compost—
now dashing past the old Volvo, uncoil the green hose,
cleaning a car in the rain, after all
it's not a downpour, just enough
to shiver the daffodils, tall
in their pots on the landing, eight bright
trumpets, their charge of yellow cheering me on—
to the woodpile next,
chunks of oak and madrone,
an armful up the stairs—
to the hearth, though the hamper's
loaded, it could rain all day
and anyway, my whole body's rejoicing—
all tools at hand—
crumpled paper,
a little kindling, and as the flames go up,
the kettle to fill,
green tea
in a glass mug,
my hands around the heat,
and as the drumming on the roof
crescendoes,
catching my breath,
at last!
listen to the rain.

In the Raspberry Patch

The earth is soft after rain.
My small pitchfork digs in, uprooting
the oxalis. I toss its clovery
greens, flimsy yellow blossoms, thrill
to uncover, at the base of stiff brown
canes, each new sprig of the saw-toothed
raspberry. And at the fringes, in the path,
even under the fence invading the iris—
all the little renegades!
They could easily take over. I leap
to transplant them, fumbling
for the trowel, almost
in summer now
tasting raspberries.

The Blue Sky at Pinnacles Again

We'd come in spring, young
in our marriage, seeking out the first yellow violets,
the trickle of creek at the start of the trail,
Indian paintbrush higher up,
you with your camera leading the way, knowing the names
from the wildflower book,
left behind today and suddenly missed,
like your hand around mine.

They're still here, these immense ruddy rocks
with their sculpted shapes, rounded and quiet,
long settled in, each dewy shadow at their base
bringing miners' lettuce, milk-maids, the surprise of early
shooting-stars—and still, near these old lava-flows, so close to
unchanging, my heart beats quickly on the steep ascent.

After Three Thousand Saturdays

It's sweet to curl up,
nest again,
breath deepening
almost to a doze—
and then a little whisper, *belly,*
belly, belly, gets me up laughing.
Sure enough,
it's my eight-year-old imp-face
in the mirror,
the same brightness
beaming through the wrinkles.
What's happened to the achy
knees, fingers? This
body's so limber could be any
new creature, wiggling baby
gopher out of its hole, another spring
morning, a mother's voice
calling up the stairs,
Little bird, to her fledgling
just waking, wide open.

Finishing
    for J. (1914—1998)

I pull the back door open
to the light and the plum trees' blossoming,
start to pound tiny nails in a bookcase.
A deep breath of sea air—
your birthday.
                Once, in a doorway,
your blue eyes beamed as the dark
took you, raving—tiny tumor in one eye
spreading to that beautiful tree, your brain—
you dreamed yourself away,
small boat on a river
drifting out to the China Sea
in the arms of Quan Yin.
                Now,
for your hand I last held, steadying,
up a muddy path for a glimpse of the sea,
for the dream of you, who came to me in the mountains,
young and light, showering love
in a radiant nakedness—
                in this doorway,
open to the sun, to the sea, to the plum trees' blossoming,
for you, these tiny finishing nails,
warm in the palm of my hand.

After Turning off the News of War
for Christine

Hot sun on our backs, we pry up
the stepping stones, weed the edges,
shovel old wood chips into buckets,
pull up black matting in shreds. We're clearing
and widening the path from the lemon tree
to the gate. You find a soldier beetle, orange
helmet, black stripe down each wing,
antennae waving. *One of the good bugs,*
aphid-eaters. I bring glasses of water.
We sit on the edge of the deck
to drink in the pepper tree's shade.
A bench would be nice here, you remind me,
and then we speak of birthdays, choices
of cake and frosting, recipes that call for
the darkest, most bittersweet chocolate.

Night Heron
for Ed

I.
Out my window, too big to perch on a wire,
flown to the neighbor's peaked roof—what is that bird?
Black-crowned head. Thick orange beak.
So rare, we thought, that one you stalked, summers ago
around the lagoon at dusk.

A crow comes flapping and that amazing neck
elongates even further. Those deep brown wing feathers
ruffle the crow off. Let's say a *she* tilts her head
in a wide apricot yawn.

Porch door bangs, she hunches down like a duck,
twists her neck to peck her own back,
then flicks tail feathers,
walks to the gutter edge,
tucks one leg under,
and peers around.

Doesn't look hurt.
What is she waiting for? She lifts
and pulls her wings together high on her back,
crouches, claws curled
over the edge, breast like a ship's
prow, and nestles into the gutter.

Now she darts down to the weeds,
and I go out to see—
Oh—the fish.
All those missing koi.

II.
I keep watch in the garden that evening.
I lie in wait, flat on the little dock. She lands
close, by the lemon tree, moves toward the shallow edge.
I leap up shrieking, flapping my arms,
and throw the tarp over her fishing hole.

When the fish swim out now,
it's to the wide middle,
and in the air above
there's only a pale blue dragonfly.

Rest in This

A few pink streaks low in the east
the sea fog rolls in—
let it pull you
away from the buzz
of motors and news
barefoot to the cliff
down the wooden steps
to the mudstone shelf
soothing to touch
then watch along the fog's edge
a kayak barely moving
parallel to shore.

Sit.
You once knew stillness—
breathe it in
let the ribs of a shell
brush the back of your hand
puffs of wind
on your cheek
and the sun's
increasing warmth.
Close your eyes
and listen
to the length of every wave.

In the Blink of an Eye

We were fresh from the toystore
with our new stuffed animals
and the flowerman full of his arrangings,
bending over his buckets of iris and daisies.

He said no, we could not have
four separate differently colored flowers, one
for each of us including the animals,
no, only by the dozen.
So I said, *Okay, then. You choose, Gus.*

Together we found the biggest, the freshest bunch,
and over the purples and pinks of their petals,
the yellows of their centers, the green
saw-toothed edges of their leaves ruffling,
I read the black letters on the white paper
aloud—RAINBOW ASTERS
ESPECIALLY LONG LASTING $1.50—
Rainbow Asses?!
We laughed with the flowerman,
you with your yellow hair
the only daffodil.
You were four

and now here we go again,
stuffed squirrel, frog, even a monkey,
flowers filling the house
and your mother crooning *oh those big black eyes*—
you're a father!

Saturdays

A whiff of eggs and bacon,
my red plaid shirt with snaps, blue jeans that
zip up the side—I'm running downstairs,
my mother's laughing, still in her apron,
on her tiptoes for the picnic basket,
my father's calling from the basement stairs,
already pulling his high-tops on,
my brothers scrambling in the hall closet for theirs.
I grab my toast—strawberry jam—
We're going!
               We're on the running board
into the velvety back of the old blue Chrysler,
past the putting greens, the cemetery, over
the Tittabawassee on its bumpy bridge,
to the straight gravel road by fields and woods, and on
to the turn at last—the new green sign
to our farm! Split rail fences, first apple trees,
past Shad and Mary's paint-peeled shack,
up the little hill by the root cellar
here's the farm bell on its post, the yellow-brick house,
the old red barns, the silvery silo—
forty acres, pine woods beyond—
the sweet dry smell of hay, the steamy
stench of manure, and now, for us, the white-plumed
whinnies of horses.

After Miss Shelley, Miss Hattersley, Miss Guilford—

When I can't remember the name of my third grade teacher,
the only one through ninth grade
that won't spring to mind, I sit
wondering at the mystery of her.
Like a fan blowing cool air in summer, her face
bends down to me, strands of her hair—
it must have been long—or the rayony
swish of her skirt lightly brushing my arm
as my pen writes the letters very precisely, rounding them
in the new cursive, her voice a glissando
tinseled with laughter, her eyes crinkling—
the one who left to get married!—
up there behind her glasses,
the glow of her.

Old South School

The sidewalk my feet once knew in every weather
still heads straight
to the corner of Martin's drugstore,
still turns north on Elm, where
the white-belted boys on safety patrol
held their arms out for us, past the red and white pole
at Mickey's, king of crewcuts,
and stops at the little flight of steps,
plinth of chipped concrete by the kindergarten door—
locked. It's summer, and all the windows
now stuccoed muddy brown,
so even when the kids are at their desks,
they can't see out.

I want my yellow slicker,
my locker by the art room stairs
where once in a morning of thunder,
from the stairwell's high window
dark clouds blew away
and just in time
for walking home
the sun poured down.

A crow now,
flapping and cawing high above the west steps,
and there, on top of the entrance columns, stone claws
clinging to the eaves—tiny gargoyles grinning.

Killarney Beach

The air soars with birdcalls, sparrows darting.
Nothing holds still. Even the path
curves, its sand swirled in patterns—footprints
mingle with the shadows of the wind-tossed grasses—
edge of beach at the bay,
the warm hollows we'd run to, wet after swimming,
burrow in under the wind-blown sumac—me, my brothers,
and those little red-headed, freckle-faced boys
we went fishing with, the Ayers from the cottage next door.
There we all are in front of the rowboat—
my brother, just turned six, holding up our little string of perch,
me wearing my necklace of shells and my pink bathing suit
with the hole in the middle so my tummy showed.

I'd like to stay with these sparrows
in the Queen Anne's lace—one sways
from the tallest still-green blossom, swivels
upside down—tiny black-striped head bobbing,
pecks the new seeds.

That next summer when we come, the first seaweedy
shore smells, billows of wind as we tumble from the car,
running to find them, those friendly, freckled boys I could race with,
maybe hug—at the screened door of their cottage, unfamiliar voices . . .

IV.

The Root Tree Dreams

Night After Night

We drive around the island
Our hands turn to bone
on the wheel
No blood
but what this body's lost
will ever bind us
The waters rise
a blur of blue above the windows
The running boards dissolve
The babies sink
beneath us
Without bitterness
let me go down to them

The Root Tree Dreams
Green Dragon Temple, Green Gulch Farm, 1996-1997

Fall

A flurry of leaves, crisp red underfoot.
The teahouse is closed.
We hike to the dock, eat lunch in the ferryhouse.
A bell rings. I'm missing my water bottle,
my knapsack is open and empty—
no, here's the black wallet,
address book.
                Everybody's left.
A last look around the room.
Through the long underground passage,
I see the stairs.
                I'm going back
to my childhood bedroom—a simple, single bed—
and my mother. I'm aware she's dead.
I try on nightgowns, one pink, one blue,
choose the Blackwatch plaid
I sleep in now.
                Dark of the moon and I'm lost—a vast
ocean-edge of dunes, tidelands, on my knees in the sand,
when a voice—*Search for past wisdom!*—
wakes me.
                * * *

The room is bathed in earliest light.
Three Egyptian figures on a frieze
move left along a wall into the shadow
of a rock that opens as they enter.
I hear one word: *curator.*

When I fall asleep again,
there's the wide open face of a baby,

and I'm back in the car with Ed,
my young estranged husband, driving, my hand
stroking his head. His fingers meet mine,
I kiss his ear lobe.

I wake with the bell in the dark before dawn,
take my place among the black-robed,
find my shadow on the wall.
All the years to sit with, knees aching,
listening to an old conversation:

> *I don't know how to stop it.*
> *I'll go away from here.*
> A softer voice says,
> "*You have all you need.*"
> *What is it I need?*
> "*Peace.*"
> *I've got to get there*
> carrying heartache like a baby.
> *And then we drove up to Fione, just the two of us.*
> A castle. *He wants to go.* Left eye hurting. *I say no* . . .
> *Let's just sit here, side by side, and talk.*
> So simple. Would that have taken care of it?
> *Your father has you trapped up front, I see.*
> So old, frail. The sadness sinking in,
> that he'll be gone.

* * *

That night I'm driving a car-boat at dusk,
my father in the passenger seat, lake air on our faces,
when out of the woods our black dog comes rushing to meet us,
veers, plunges into the lake. *Come back!* I call out,
but now we're walking on swampy ground,

my father's stumbling in his black dress-shoes,
he can't see, sits down in a sink-hole
and goes under. I reach in, catch one arm, lift
until his head's above the muddy water.

At last the hero appears in a school for boys.
He's written several fine essays on Shakespeare.
A sunny hero, highest in his class, he's in charge
of the water in a low kingdom, discovers it's about to
burst in a flood he can't stop. He sounds the alarm, barely
escapes, water breaks through the walls, other boys
scramble to contain it, start to flee across the bridge—
the force of the river surging beneath
explodes upward.

* * *

Hot sun by the pond. I'm sitting,
bees adrift in the last purple thistle.
With each puff of wind, wisps of white down
blow from the dry stalks.
Out on the rippled water, a great blue heron,
motionless so long my eyes close
and when I look again,
the sun's too bright to find him.
So, flown without me, and I'm almost turning
when the immense wings lift.

> Tears, and the whole body eased,
> as if a door opened
> from the other side.
> A place to rest.
> *There are wildflowers here, leaves.*
>
> *What are you doing, honey?*
> A voice like my grandmother's.

* * *

Box elders. German nails. Our old family doctor is coming to call,
climbing the stairs with his hypodermics and all I can do is
wake up, shaking in a sweat—
years of bronchitis, how I hated those shots!—
go to the window and look at the stars.

Clothes washing. All morning
warm, soft air, a high wind in the trees,
unseasonably balmy.
Lying by the pond, dry weeds
and earth under me,
my body and the earth the same.

Winter

> *Bruised facts.*
> *The Sorrow House.*
> *A loose dance with some courage in it.*

I dream of running east along old Gratiot Road,
a white towel around my body,
another around my head.
I'm running to get home on that country road,
yet pass our house, find myself in town,
a street dimly lit, crowded with stores.
Now, close to me, a wide-faced woman in a wheel-chair
tells me: *I died falling.*
I'd like to have died
in childbirth.
The dark, wee hours,
raining hard on the roof.
By morning, hands, arms, shoulders—all softened.

No harsh self-accusations. Just this
deep, effortless breathing.

> *I know each rising and falling.*
> Still, hours sitting
> until, just before the bell,
> the whole hurt left side of my body
> moves all at once into the center to meet the right—
> such a welling-up of relief, asking, *What is it?*
> a high clear voice piping,
> *Life, life!*
> Then an older voice:
> *. . . come and gone through nothing.*
> *There's a circle in here*
> *called Bethlehem.*
> That little family, the one I first knew,
> the baby in a manger,
> animals around,
> wise men on their knees.

I fly north to the valley surrounded by mountains,
constant snow falling,
the streets no sooner plowed
than covered, still falling as we run the last blocks
to church, Christmas night,
lungs full of snow-air, old carols.
Later, a lone deer.

Back on the coast, endless warm rain,
the sky gray, hills green from so much wet,
and up the firetrail between downpours,
close among the trunks of eucalyptus,
three fawns in the rain-light.

Shaky, I wake three times in the night:
I don't know where I'm going.
It takes days to remember.

               * * *

Meanwhile, the hero, bearded, middle-aged now,
hacks at straw. The message: *what needs attending to is
around the left ear,* and then someone tearing his ear off.
Later, boats at sea in the night, and he's overboard,
struggling underwater, all the toes and front pads of his left foot
ripped off. Whatever happened to Shakespeare?

> *Gum-slow and headstrong
> at the same time.*

Sitting in silence, seven days of rain.
Then, a slice of moon in the dark before dawn,
flashes of sunlight after breakfast,
no wind yet in the trees, so I'm drawn out,
up the firetrail—rivulets, waterfalls, the creek rushing white,
and higher up, near the dark rain-glistened trunks of the live oak,
stalks of tiny white lily-of-the-valley and the bright
chirruping of a bird . . .

> *What you've most hidden away . . .
> all the beautiful boys.   Drop down deep
> to the interior spine. Just listen.
> Twisted singing.
> Great effort.*

Cold early morning with stars,
big winds thrash the trees
and where the porch-light glimmers—enormous dark
wings lift suddenly from ground to roof-peak.

The great horned head swivels.

> *Anxiety. About what's next.*
> *There isn't enough . . . time.*

Spring

Tonight in my house three men all
want me: Robin, in plaid flannel pajamas,
pants in the living room, a stocky, black-haired
and bearded younger man, says *here, between*
my thighs, and I go to the one waiting in the bedroom,
curly butternut hair and beard, already
naked, face down on the sheets, starting without me.
I jump in.
Wake up wanting more.

> *Great root tree, root blossoms.*
> *I don't know what happened to him.*
> *We are working things out for you through the Ancestors.*
> Or did they say, *We are working the Ancestors out*
>   *through you?*

Now that rejected old boyfriend. His younger
brother offers me chocolate at a party, gets
mad that I won't dance. He's after me and I'm hiding out
in my parents' bathroom, wrapped in the white towel,
thighs naked, dark crotch showing, and my thumb
pushing the button on the doorknob that won't
lock. The door springs open
and there's only a pale-faced workman, in glasses,
kneeling in his jeans, repairing my parents' bedroom floor.

* * *

We kneel in our black robes,
offer incense to remember the babies who died—
each story told—of the still-born,
the miscarried, the aborted—
all the tiny red Buddha bibs sewn,
held near an altar in the garden,
lifted to flutter from a tree of their own.

That night I'm lost in a strange city, a slum
apartment where an old man
and a dark-haired woman want to see
the photographs I'm carrying near my heart—
photos Ed's taken,
one of a river edged in willows,
one close-up of himself floating naked on the water,
his pubic hair glowing a burnished red-gold.
The dark-haired woman
wants to know how big his penis is.
The old man spits on the photos.
I grab a rolled-up Sunday *Times*,
the old man's picture on the front page,
throw the whole paper out the window.

Coming of age . . . to age.

A night-long conversation
flying body to body with a tall young man.
His face above mine says,
Your whole mouth and chin look softer now.

This little book of S.O.S.

* * *

Time to bathe, pay bills, then hike
up the high coast trail, write to nephew and niece:
noon-sun on the ocean, shimmering,
wind in the tall spring grasses,
fluttering the poppies,
shaking the coyote-brush—
shadows shift and play over lichened rock.

O Light that we turn to
between the wind's gusts,
be warm, draw us nearer you
when our bodies' warmth leaves.

Wherever we go,
in the marsh-meadow
there'll be a white horse and a chestnut
nuzzling, and if it's spring
someone will take the turn
into the boxhedge garden,
and find, behind the lilacs,
the prickery barberry,
tiny red leaves just sprouting.

You haven't lost language, says the teacher.

>   On a single stalk, white blossoms—
>   *for such a small flower, what fragrance!*
>   and then three ripe
>   strawberries.

Ethics, cleaning, and strawberries.

* * *

And so it's April,
I'm dreaming of Ginny, my earliest friend,
on horseback with her child.
I'm walking beside them through the woods,
then left behind,
climbing through hillsides of poison-oak,
calling, *Come back!*

Then no landscape at all,
only standing close to Ed when a huge
snake darts its head into my face,
wraps its tail around our feet,
binds us to the ground.

Summer

I'm asleep,
standing close to Ed again—
this time his body melts into mine,
then grows taller in the distance on a mountain.
I see his head circled in sunlight,
my youngest nephew sheltered under the crook of his arm.

> *Translucent pain.*
> *Torch of tranquility.*

The first fog drifts in, early morning of the ceremony—
soon I'll kneel with the new Bodhisattvas,
we'll take our vows to free all beings.
I dress for the ceremony and wonder
who is taking these vows?

The next day I sleep in,
far from the black robes, beyond the bell—
a clearing in the woods.
Hands draw me in and I'm chosen,
kissed, hugged by a man my age . . .

I find Ed in his new house.
He has a room with three beds—
our old queen-sized,
one of the twins my brothers slept in as boys,
and from my girlhood, the apple-green French provincial,
peach roses in the headboard.
The room is filled with fruit trees,
grape vines, melon patches, berry bushes.
On one tree, cherries, Ed's favorite,
grow on the same branch with apples, mine.
We'll never be able to eat all this.

I wake up laughing.

Rowboat

You in the stern, Ed,
your new baby, Amelia, alone in the bow,
and I in the water, undoing
the rope.
           We shove off, but the boat
nosedives, and we
plunge to the bottom.
                  We can talk
underwater, calling
back and forth, *Over here!*
I see her!
          At last
you reach her, float her
to me, and I, catching,
buoy her up and up—
into the sunshine, splashing.

The Deer at Santa Sabina
January 2002

Mid-day, a misty rain in the nuns' garden.
Four deer stand close together
licking each others' ears, necks, faces.
The youngest is getting a full body scrub.
Every few licks, its mother's long neck turns
so her tongue can reach her own back.
A hoof lifts to scratch a muzzle.
                                         Heads lift,
ears fan, and for long moments
they wait, listening. Then tongues flick down
into fur again.
                       One breaks away,
steps over the glistening ground,
nibbles at a single bright leaf
among the newly fallen from the sweet-gum
and very slowly eats it.
                             All the deer are still now.
The rain keeps falling.

Rosie King was born in Saginaw, Michigan. A graduate of Wellesley College, she came west in 1966 and did her master's degree at San Francisco State and her doctorate in literature at UC Santa Cruz. Her poetry was first honed as she taught beginning poets and wrote a dissertation on the poetry of H.D. She has practiced and taught Rosen bodywork for over twenty years and lived for six years as a Zen monk at Green Gulch and Tassajara. She makes her home, with pond, fruit trees, and garden, near the beach in Santa Cruz. *Sweetwater, Saltwater* is her first book.